Penguin

Pair Work One

Student A

Peter Watcyn-Jones

PENGUIN ENGLISH

PENGUIN BOOKS

Published by the Penguin Group
Penguin Books Ltd, 27 Wrights Lane, London W8 5TZ, England
Penguin Books USA Inc., 375 Hudson Street, New York, New York 10014, USA
Penguin Books Australia Ltd, Ringwood, Victoria, Australia
Penguin Books Canada Ltd, 10 Alcorn Avenue, Toronto, Ontario, Canada M4V 3B2
Penguin Books (NZ) Ltd, 182–190 Wairau Road, Auckland 10, New Zealand

Penguin Books Ltd, Registered Offices: Harmondsworth, Middlesex, England

First published 1984
10 9 8 7 6

Typeset, printed and bound in Great Britain by
BPCC Hazell Books
Aylesbury, Bucks, England
Member of BPCC Ltd.
Set in Bembo

Contents

To the teacher

Pair Work One forms part of the Penguin Functional English course and was written to give students, working in pairs, further practice in the structures and functions introduced in *First Impact*. The book can, however, be used equally successfully with any other existing functionally-based course at pre-intermediate level.

Description of the material

Like its predecessor, *Pair Work*, *Pair Work One* consists of two books, one for Student A and the other for Student B. [*Pair Work* is similar to *Pair Work One* but is intended for more advanced students (intermediate level and upwards). Included in the introduction to the teacher in that book is the rationale behind using two books instead of one.]

Each book contains thirty-one activities. These are arranged, where possible, into pairs of activities, so that if Student A has one particular role or task in the first activity, then he or she has Student B's role or task in the second, and vice versa. This gives both students practice in the same structure or function, but avoids the possibly boring alternative of simply changing parts and doing exactly the same activity again. Instead of this, the same structure or function is practised again, but the situation (or role) is changed. However, if the teacher and the group would like to repeat activities then there is no reason, of course, why students shouldn't change books and do them again. But this is probably best done at a later date.

The activities can be divided into four main types:

1   Simulations/role-plays
The main difference between a simulation and a role-play is that, in the former, students play themselves but are given a definite task to do or are put in a specific situation and asked to make appropriate responses, whereas in the latter, students are given definite roles to play and are usually asked to assume a different name, background, and so on. An example of a simulation is Activity 14 – For sale, while an example of a role-play is Activity 11 – Newspaper interview (1).

2   One-sided dialogues
These are activities in which students read a dialogue together but can see only their own part, which usually includes opportunities for the student to make his or her own responses. An example of a one-sided dialogue is Activity 26 – Shopping.

3   Information-transfer activities
These are activities in which students are asked to perform a task together; they fall into two types. In the first, one student has access to all the information and tries to impart it to his or her partner. An example of this type is Activity 20 – Complete the drawing (1).

In the second, both students are given access to half the information and, by working together, try to solve the whole. An example of this type is Activity 22 – The life of Elvis Presley.

4   Questionnaires or discussion/conversation activities
These are activities designed to stimulate students to discuss a subject or subjects

with their partner, and usually take the form of a questionnaire. These activities are particularly useful when students are practising giving opinions and showing agreement or disagreement. An example of this type of activity is Activity 4 – Questionnaire: likes and dislikes.

How to use the books

The activities in *Pair Work One* have been written to give extra practice in certain structures and functions. Consequently, they should be done as follow-up work rather than for 'teaching' purposes, since the books assume that the student has a basic knowledge of structures plus the language needed to perform the various functions.

In the Appendix (pages 54–64), a list of the structures and functions for each activity is given, plus examples of typical questions, sentences or responses. Using this as a guide, all the teacher has to do is to decide which structure or function needs practising and choose an appropriate activity from the ones given. Since, in many instances, more than one activity has been written to practise a particular structure or function, repeated practice can be given without the students becoming bored.

Finally, since the level throughout the books is pre-intermediate, there is no need to take the activities in order if the needs of the class and the teacher dictate otherwise. Indeed, it is not envisaged that the books should be worked through from beginning to end: the activities can, and should, be taken in any order depending on the needs of a particular class.

Teaching hints

1 Classroom organization

Since the activities in *Pair Work One* involve the students working in pairs, a certain amount of classroom reorganization may be necessary. If it is at all possible, the room should be arranged in such a way that pairs face one another across a desk or a table. This is to give them 'eye-contact' which makes communication a lot easier. Again, if possible, some sort of screen (e.g. a bag) should be placed between them so that they cannot see one another's books.

However, there may be practical reasons why such a classroom arrangement may not be possible, in which case the teacher can adapt the working methods accordingly to suit his or her particular circumstances.

2 Working in pairs

Since the students will be working in pairs, there is the inevitable problem of what happens when there is an odd number of students in the class. Here are one or two possible solutions (although they are by no means the only ones):

a. The teacher forms the 'extra' partner, in which case he or she should choose a different student to work with each time.

b. The 'odd' student monitors another pair. The student chosen to monitor another pair should be changed each time an activity is done.

c. Three students work together instead of two. Two of the students form a team to partner the third one, taking it in turns to talk to him or her. Again, the group of three should be changed frequently.

One final consideration regarding pair work is that partners should be changed frequently to ensure that everyone really gets an opportunity to work with and to get to know as many different members of the class as possible.

3 Introducing an activity

Clear instructions are given for all the activities, so in most cases it should be sufficient for the teacher simply to ask the students to turn to a particular activity and to let them read through the instructions. While they do this, the teacher goes around the class checking that they have fully understood what they have to do before they begin.

If, on the other hand, the class lacks confidence or is not used to communicative work, the teacher could, on the first few occasions when the book is used, demonstrate briefly with two students (A and B) while the class monitor them. Alternatively, the teacher could set up the situation with the whole class then, by prompting the students, get suggestions as to what A and B might say to each other.

Whichever method is chosen, it is essential that the students know *exactly* what they have to do before they are allowed to begin.

4 Working through an activity

It is probably better if all pairs start working at the same time rather than working one after the other. During the activity, the teacher moves from pair to pair, as a passive observer, noting problems or mistakes which can be taken up with the whole group afterwards.

The length of the activities varies from approximately five to twenty minutes. It is up to the teacher and the class to decide whether to spend a whole lesson on the activities or else to make them a part of the normal lesson. (Perhaps a combination of these two is a good idea.)

Finally, since not all groups will finish at exactly the same time, it may be necessary for the teacher to have a definite 'finishing time' in mind for some of the more open-ended activities.

5 Following up an activity

The teacher should always spend a few minutes after an activity discussing it with the class. The discussion could include talking about what the students found difficult as well as finding out if anyone wanted to say something but didn't have the necessary language to express himself or herself. This is also the time when any mistakes can be pointed out and, if necessary, revision practice given.

Finally, it is a good idea occasionally to ask one of the pairs to practise the activity again while the rest of the class listen and monitor their performance.

6 Activity 1 and Activity 2

Although these two activities practise asking and answering questions, the chief reason for putting them first in the book is that they are a useful way of breaking the ice when the class is a new one – although they are still useful even when the class has been together for some time.

Getting to know you (1)

Get to know something about Student B by asking him/her questions and filling in the following form. (Student B will also ask you questions.)

Name: .... Age: ....

Country of origin: .... Nationality: ....

Home town/village: ....

Number of people in family: ....

Mother	Father	Number of brothers	Number of sisters	Anyone else
☐	☐	....	....	....

Father's occupation: ....

Mother's occupation ....

Still at school   Yes/No   Left school: .... (*year*)

(If Student B has left school):

Present job: ....

or

College/University: ....

Length of time spent studying English: .... years

Interests: ....

....

Favourite colour: ....

Foreign countries visited: ....

Main ambition: ....

Before starting, work out which questions to ask. For example:

What's your name?
Where do you come from?
Have you got any brothers?
What's your father's job?
How long have you been studying English?

When you have finished, use the answers Student B gave you to fill in the gaps in the following sentences.

1 I spoke to ....

2 He/She is ....years old and comes from ....

3 He/She is .... (*nationality*) and lives in a town/village

   called ....

4 There are .... people in his/her family altogether – his/her ....

   ....

5 His/Her father is a/an .... and his/her mother

   is a/an ....

6 He/She is still at school.

OR He/She left school in 19.... and is now studying at ....

   .... (*name of College/University*)

OR He/She left school in 19.... and is now working as a/an ....

7 He/She has been studying English for .... years.

8 His/Her interests are ....

   .... and his/her favourite colour is ....

9 He/She hasn't visited any foreign countries.

OR The only foreign country he/she has visited is ....

OR He/She has visited ....

   .... (*names of foreign countries*).

10 Finally, his/her main ambition is to ....

   ....

When you have finished, find another partner. Now tell this person all about Student B by reading out the sentences above.

2 Getting to know you (2)

Ask Student B questions to find out the things below. Before starting, work out which questions to ask. (Student B will also ask you questions.)

Find out if Student B:	Yes	No	Other Information
1 is afraid of the dark. (Are you . . .?)			
2 is married. (If the answer is Yes, find out what Student B's wife/husband is called)			
3 is good at sport.			
4 lives in a town or a village (Do you . . .?)			
5 always does his/her homework.			
6 goes home by bus.			
7 has got a dog or a cat. (Have you got . . .?)			
8 has got more than two brothers. (If the answer is Yes, find out how many brothers Student B has got)			
9 has got any relatives in England.			
10 can swim. (Can you . . .?)			
11 can speak more than two languages. (If the answer is Yes, find out which languages Student B can speak)			
12 was born in May or June. (If the answer is Yes, find out on which day Student B was born) (Were you . . .?)			
13 started school before he/she was seven. (Did you . . .?)			
14 listened to the radio last night. (If the answer is Yes, find out the name of one of the programmes Student B listened to)			
15 has been to Scotland. (Have you . . .?)			
16 has had more than two boyfriends/girlfriends.			
17 is going abroad next summer. (If the answer is Yes, find out where Student B is going) (Are you going . . .?)			
18 would like to be a millionaire. (Would you . . .?)			

When you have finished, find another partner. Now tell him/her what you found out about Student B.

3 Missing information: the Eurovision Song Contest

A daily newspaper is publishing each day a short description of some of the singers taking part in the Eurovision Song Contest. Here is today's list of singers. Unfortunately, some of the information about them is missing. Ask Student B questions to find out the missing information and fill it in. (Student B also has missing information and will ask you questions.)

You can ask questions like these:

> How old is . . . (say name)?
> Where does . . . (say name) . . . live?
> Which country is . . . (say name) . . . singing for?
> Is . . . (say name) . . . married or single?
> How long has . . . (say name) . . . been a pop singer?
> What are . . . (say name)'s interests?
> What is the name of the song . . . (say name) . . . is going to sing?
> What is . . . (say name)'s ambition?

Who's who in the Eurovision Song Contest   Part 2

Name	Maria Rossi		Astrid Klempe	
Age	35			
Home town			Hamburg	
Country			Germany	
Married/single	married			
Length of time as a pop singer				
Interests	music .... painting		yoga .... horses	
Song title (in English)	You Alone			
Ambition			To meet Rod Stewart	

10

Name	Fleming Larsen		Paula Allen	
Age	30			
Home town	Copenhagen			
Country	Denmark		Ireland	
Married/single			single	
Length of time as a pop singer			2 years	
Interests	.... fishing......		bird-watching ballet.......... cooking	
Song title (in English)	Rocking Through The Night			
Ambition			To get married and have lots of children	

Name	'Nana'		Marcel Meyer	
Age	25			
Home town			Paris	
Country	Greece		France	
Married/single	married			
Length of time as a pop singer	4 years			
Interests	tennis...... dogs......		.... golf............. song-writing	
Song title (in English)	Love Me Tonight		Jeannette	
Ambition	To be rich and famous			

When you have finished, check with Student B to see if you have filled in the missing information correctly.

(NOTE: The Eurovision Song Contest is a competition held once a year by the various television companies in Europe to pick the best pop song. There is a jury in each country who gives marks for each song and the song with the highest total is the winner. The competitors from each country must sing the song in the language of their country.)

4 Questionnaire: likes and dislikes

Work on your own. Read through the following sentences and choose an answer (I like, I quite like, I don't like, I hate, etc.). Mark your answer with a cross (×).

I love	I like	I quite like	I don't really like	I don't like	I hate	
						listening to pop music.
						cats.
						writing letters.
						horror films (*Dracula*, *Frankenstein*, etc.)
						this town.
						being alone.
						cooking.
						ice-cream.
						the smell of garlic.
						singing.
						modern furniture.
						watching football.
						washing my hair.
						our teacher.
						flying.
						my school (or my job).
						getting up early.
						going to discos.
						visiting relatives.
						talking about myself.

When you have finished, find a partner (Student B). Now talk about your likes and dislikes like this:

You:	I quite like listening to pop music.	
Student B:	Yes, so do I/Yes, me too. OR Oh, I don't. (I hate it.)	
Student B:	I don't like washing my hair.	
You:	No, neither do I. OR Oh, I do. (I love it.)	

Take it in turns to start.

5 Who's who?

Here are six people plus some information about them:

| | | Peter | | | |

Peter is a year older than Sally.
Mary is fatter than both Julie and Sally.
John is twenty-one next birthday.
The tallest person is a year younger than John.
Julie is the oldest – she is three years older than Mary.

Student B also has information about the six people. Work together to see if you can work out their names and their ages. (Write them in the boxes.)

You are allowed to read out the information you have about the six people *but you must not let Student B see your book.*

6 One-sided dialogue: making suggestions

Student B is your friend. Today is Friday. You are discussing where to go tomorrow. Unfortunately, you can see only your part of the dialogue so you must listen carefully to what Student B says. Use the *Saturday Guide* on the opposite page when trying to decide where to go.

Before you start, read through your part to have some idea of what you will say. When you are both ready you can begin.

You: Shall we do something tomorrow, . . . (*say Student B's name*)? I don't really feel like staying in again.

Student B: . . .

You: I'm not sure really. Perhaps there's something in the newspaper – in the *Saturday Guide*.

Student B: . . .

You: What?

Student B: . . .

You: No, I don't really like watching . . . (*name the sport*)

Student B: . . .

You: Where to?

Student B: . . .

You: I'd rather not. (*Explain that travelling for hours in a coach makes you feel sick*)

Student B: . . .

You: Why don't we go to an exhibition?

Student B: . . .

You: There's one on . . . (*say what the two exhibitions are about*)

Student B: . . .

You: Well, it was only a suggestion.

Student B: . . .

You: (*Ask what time it starts*)

Student B: . . .

You: All right. Let's do that, then.

Student B: . . .

SATURDAY GUIDE

Sports Events

Indoor Football

Finals of the South
of England indoor
football
competition
for schools.
Leisure Centre
Kick-off: 10.30
Final: approx. 4.15

Admission 50p

Water-polo

International match
between England and
Wales.

Lansdown swimming
baths 2 p.m.–
5 p.m.

Admission £1

Judo

National
championships
for women.

Wigmore Sports
Centre 1.30–4.30

Admission 60p

Exhibitions

18th-century Landscape Paintings

Exhibition of
eighteenth-century
landscape paintings
by well-known local
artists.

Grover Art Gallery
10–5.30

Admission 80p

Scandinavian Design

Exhibition of modern
furniture from
Denmark, Sweden
and Finland.

Design Centre
1.30–4.30

Admission Free

Excursions

Isle of Wight and Stonehenge

Coach tour to the Isle
of Wight and Stonehenge.
Depart: 7.30 from
Station Road.
Arrive back:
approx. 9.30 p.m.

Cost £2.50
(including lunch)

The Motor Show

Special coach trip
to the Motor Show
at Earls Court, London.
Depart: 9.15 from
Station Road.
Arrive back:
approx. 8.15 p.m.

Cost £4.50
(including lunch
and admission)

Other Events

A Midsummer Night's Dream

Special open-air
performance of
one of Shakespeare's
best-loved
plays by students
of Brindly Drama
School.

Singleton Park
2.30 p.m.

Seats £1.50

Cat Show

Local cat show at
St Peter's Church
Hall. 9.30–5.30

Admission 20p

Computer Fair

See and try out the
latest in home
computers. Special
attraction for children –
Games Corner – a chance
to play the latest
computer games.

Wigmore Conference Centre 10–6 p.m.

Admission adults £1 children 50p

15

7 Following instructions (1)

Here is a rectangle which contains twenty squares. You are going to write or draw something in fifteen of them. Student B will tell you what to draw or write and in which squares. But it is not as easy as it sounds, so you will have to listen very carefully to his/her instructions.

1	2	3	4	5
6	7	8	9	10
11	12	13	14	15
16	17	18	19	20

Before you start, make sure you have a pencil ready. If, at any time, you do not understand what Student B says, you can ask him/her to repeat the instructions (e.g. I'm sorry, I didn't understand that. Could you say it again, please?). *But you are not allowed to ask for the number of the square you are to draw or write in.*

When you have finished, compare your rectangle with Student B's to see if you have filled in everything correctly.

8 Missing information: flats and houses

Ask Student B questions to find out the missing information about the house and the flat in the table below. (Student B also has missing information and will ask you questions.)

Before you start, work out which questions to ask. For example:

> Where's (*the house*)?
> Is (*the flat*) big?
> Is (*the house*) modern?
> How many rooms are there in (*the house*)? What are they?
> Has (*the house*) got central heating?
> Is there anything else you can tell me about (*the house*)?

	Flat	House
Street	King Street	
Size	big ☐ quite big ☐ small ☐	big ☐ quite big ☑ small ☐
Condition	modern ☑ quite modern ☐ not very modern ☐	modern ☐ quite modern ☐ not very modern ☐
Number of rooms	three	*downstairs* *upstairs*
List of rooms	a living-room a kitchen a bedroom	
Central heating.	Yes	
Near the shops		No
Distance from town centre	1 mile	
Rent		£200 a month
Any other information	You share the toilet and the bathroom. On the first floor.	

When you are ready, take it in turns to ask and answer questions. When you have finished, compare your tables.

9 Following instructions (2)

On the opposite page is a rectangle which contains twenty squares. Before you start, fill in the following:

1 In square number 1 write yesterday's date.
2 In square number 4 write the colour of your hair.
3 In square number 7 write what day it will be tomorrow.
4 In square number 12 write the number 12.
5 In square number 13 write what month it is.
6 In square number 17 write the name of the capital of France.
7 In square number 19 write your name.

Now work with Student B. He/she has a large rectangle in his/her book similar to yours. But all twenty squares are empty. Help him/her to fill them in by reading out loud the following instructions. *But do not let Student B see your book.*

When you have finished, compare rectangles to see if Student B has filled in everything correctly.

Here are the instructions:

1 Start in the black square. Go down two squares. Draw a picture of a comb in this square.
2 Go right two squares. Draw a picture of a tree in this square.
3 Go up four squares. Write the colour of my hair in this square.
4 Go back to the square with the drawing of a comb. Go up one square. Draw a large circle in this square.
5 Go left one square, then up three squares. Write yesterday's date in this square.
6 In the square to the right of this, draw a picture of a bottle.
7 Go down one square, then right two squares. In this square, draw a triangle.
8 Go back to the black square. Go left one square. In this square draw a picture of a pair of glasses.
9 Go down one square. Write in this square what month it is.
10 Go right three squares. Draw a picture of an elephant in this square.
11 Go to the square to the left of the triangle. Write in this square what day it will be tomorrow.
12 Go left two squares. Draw a large cross in this square.
13 Go down three squares. In this square write the name of the capital of France.
14 Divide 144 by 12. Write your answer in the square above the drawing of the elephant.
15 Finally, write my name in the square between the drawing of the comb and the tree.

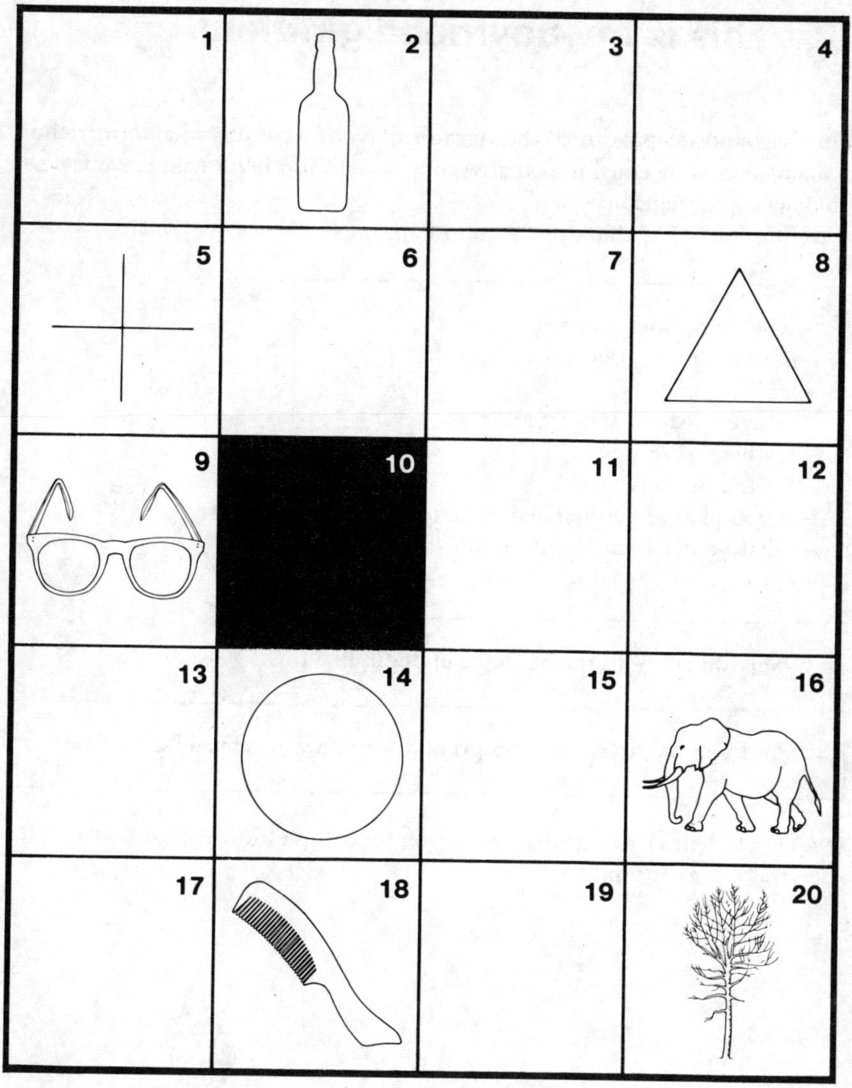
1
2
3
4
5
6
7
8
9
10
11
12
13
14
15
16
17
18
19
20

10 This is my boyfriend/girlfriend

On the opposite page is a photograph of your new boyfriend/girlfriend. Student B is your cousin. You are going to tell him/her all about your new boyfriend/girlfriend.

Before you start, think of the following:

> – where you met him/her
> – how long you have known him/her
> – his/her job
> – where he/she comes from, lives
> – his/her name, age
> – his/her interests
> – if you plan to get married (when? where?)
> – what your parents think of him/her
> etc.

When you are both ready, you can begin like this:

> Would you like to see a photograph of my new boyfriend/girlfriend?

(NOTE: Student B will probably ask you lots of questions, so be prepared to use your imagination!)

11 Newspaper interview (1)

Your name is Maria (or Rolf) Lells.

You are the leader of a Peace March which will go from Stockholm, in Sweden, to London. Here is a plan of the march and the different countries and cities you will visit on the way:

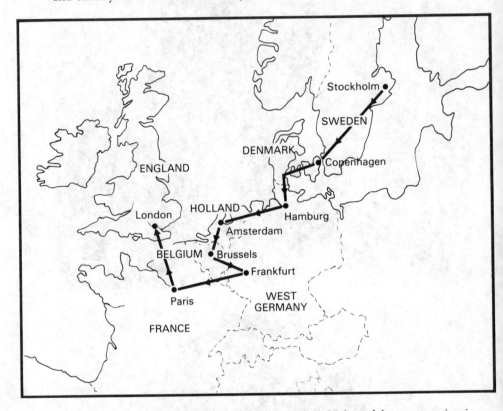

You plan to start from Stockholm on April 25th and hope to arrive in London at the end of July. You are hoping that thousands of people will join the march along the way (at least 10,000). When you get to London you are going to hold a 'Day of Peace' in Hyde Park. You are hoping that the march will show politicians that ordinary people are completely against war.

Student B is a journalist. He/she is going to interview you about the march. (Be ready to use your imagination!)

12   This is my brother

Student B is a new friend you have made on holiday. He/she is going to show you a photograph of his/her brother and his family. Find out as much as you can about them by asking Student B questions, such as:

> What's your brother's name?
> How old is he?
> What does he do?
> What's his wife's name?
> Does she go out to work too?
> How long have they been married?
> Where do they live?
> Do you see them very often?

Try to think of at least fifteen questions to ask.
When you are both ready, Student B will begin.

13 Questionnaire: habits and daily routines

Find out something about Student B's habits and daily routine by asking him/her questions. (Student B will also ask you questions.)

Before you start, work out which questions to ask. Then take it in turns to ask and answer questions. Mark Student B's answer with a cross (×).

Find out if Student B:	Yes, always	Yes, usually	Yes, often	Yes, sometimes	No, not often	No, not usually	No, hardly ever	No, never
goes out at weekends (Do you ever go . . . ?)								
remembers his/her dreams (Do you ever remember your . . . ?)								
goes to bed before 11 o'clock								
has coffee for breakfast								
does his/her homework								
comes here by bus								
catches a cold in the winter								
wears jeans to school (or work)								
feels tired in the mornings								
has lunch at a restaurant								
reads a daily newspaper								
feels nervous when he/she travels by air								
reads before he/she goes to sleep								
finds it easy to make friends								
forgets people's telephone numbers								

When you have finished, use the answers Student B gave you to fill in the missing words in the following sentences. (Remember: If Student B answered No, not often or No, not usually, you write 'He/She *doesn't often/usually* . . .')

I spoke to .... (*name*)

1 He/She .... goes out at weekends.

2 He/She .... remembers his/her dreams.

3 He/She .... goes to bed before 11 o'clock.

4 He/She .... has coffee for breakfast.

5 He/She .... does his/her homework.

6 He/She .... comes here by bus.

7 He/She .... catches a cold in the winter.

8 He/She .... wears jeans to school/work.

9 He/She .... feels tired in the mornings.

10 He/She .... has lunch at a restaurant.

11 He/She .... reads a daily newspaper.

12 He/She .... feels nervous when he/she travels by air.

13 He/She .... reads before he/she goes to sleep.

14 He/She .... finds it easy to make friends.

15 He/She .... forgets people's telephone numbers.

14 For sale

You bought the stereo cassette recorder on the opposite page three years ago for £150. You want to sell it and have put the following advertisement in the newspaper:

FOR SALE
Stereo cassette recorder.
Only three years old.
Reasonable price.
Phone 347299

Student B is going to phone you up about the cassette recorder. Before you start, look at the opposite page so that you will be able to explain all about the recorder to Student B. Also decide how much you are going to ask for it. Finally, if Student B sounds interested in buying it, arrange a day and time when he/she can come and see you.

You start like this:

Hello, 347299.

Stereo cassette recorder

built-in microphone   clock   radio with short wave, long wave, medium wave and VHF

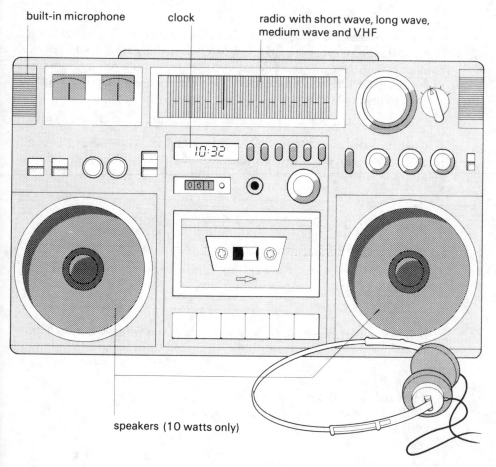

speakers (10 watts only)

Other points
also works with batteries
headphones included with it
clock can also be used as alarm clock
can record directly from radio
size: 42.5×13×26.5 cms

15 Eye-witness

You are a policeman/policewoman. Someone phoned the police station a short while ago to say that a man had stolen something from his/her shop. Student B is the person who phoned. You are going to interview him/her to try to get a description of the thief. Use the form on the opposite page.

You can begin like this:

> Good (*morning*), Sir/Madam. Now if I could just ask you one or two questions about the man who stole something from your shop this morning.

And you can end:

> Thank you very much, Sir/Madam. You've been very helpful. We'll contact you again as soon as we find him.

Before you start, work out the sort of questions you will ask. For example:

> What did the man steal?
> How old/tall was he?
> Was he fat or thin?
> What colour was his hair?
> etc.

IDENTIFICATION FORM

PB/TDY/45701

Date: ....

Name of witness: ....

Address: .... Tel. No.: ....

Crime: ....

Article(s) stolen: ....

Details of suspect

Sex	male ☐ female ☐
Age	under 18 ☐ 20–25 ☐ 26–35 ☐ 36–50 ☐ 51–60 ☐ over 60 ☐
Height	under 150 cms ☐ 150–160 cms ☐ 161–170 cms ☐ 171–180 cms ☐ 181–190 cms ☐ 191 cms–2 metres ☐ over 2 metres ☐
Build	fat ☐ well-built ☐ medium build ☐ slim ☐ thin ☐
Hair	black ☐ dark ☐ fair ☐ blond ☐ grey ☐ any other colour ....
Hairstyle	long ☐ short ☐ curly ☐ wavy ☐ straight ☐ bald ☐
Eyes	blue ☐ grey ☐ brown ☐ any other colour........................

Description of clothes

....
....
....
....
....

Any other details (beard, moustache, glasses, etc.)

....
....
....

16 Complete the crossword

The crossword on the opposite page is only half filled in. Student B also has a crossword that is only half filled in. Take it in turns to ask what the missing words are and to answer by trying to explain each word. For example:

Student B asks:	You answer:
What's 6 down?	You eat it. It's a fruit. It's yellow.
What's 10 across?	It's the opposite of 'hot'.

Before you start, work out ways of explaining the fifteen words already filled in on your crossword.

If you guess a word correctly but are not sure how to spell it, you can ask Student B to spell it for you.

When you have finished, compare your crosswords.

DOWN

ACROSS

H	O	T	E	L
		A	
		L	L
S		L
L		
T	E	L	E	V	I	S	I	O	N
P	
B	
A	N	
T	E	A	
N	E	W	S	P	A	P	E	R
P	I	L	O	T		P	O	S	
C	O	L	D	D		F	O	O	T	B	A	L	L
A	N	T	M
B	N	C	E	B	R	E	A	D
S	W	I	M
A	D

(Based on an idea by
Elizabeth Woodeson
in *MET*, Vol. 10, 1982)

17 Carry on talking

Situation 1

Here are the opening words of a conversation between two friends:

> A: You look happy, . . . (say name).
> B: Yes, I am. I had such a wonderful time last night.

Using these opening words, you are going to continue the conversation with Student B. (You will take the part of B.)
Before you start, think of what you might say. For example:

> Why did you have a wonderful time?
> Where were you? Who were you with?
> What did you do?

When you are both ready, you can begin. Student B starts.

Situation 2

Here are the opening words of another conversation between two friends:

> A: What happened to you last night? Why weren't you at the party?
> B: I'm sorry, . . . (say name), but there was trouble at home so I couldn't go.

This time, you are going to take the part of A.
Before you start, think of what you might say. For example:

> What sort of trouble did Student B have at home?
> Why didn't he/she phone to let you know he/she wouldn't be at the party?
> What was the party like? Who was there?

Try to keep the conversation going for as long as you can.
This time, you begin.

18 A family tree

Here is a drawing of a family tree. Student B also has a drawing of a family tree but it is not exactly the same as yours. (There are twelve differences.) By asking Student B questions, see if you can find the differences, and put a circle around them. Before you start, work out the sort of questions to ask. For example:

Who is Bob married to?	OR	Is Bob's wife called Alice?
What does Paul do?	OR	Is Paul a teacher?
How many children have Colin and Jennifer got?	OR	Have Colin and Jennifer got three children?
How old is Samantha?	OR	Is Samantha nineteen?

When you are both ready, take it in turns to ask and answer questions. When you have finished, compare the family trees.

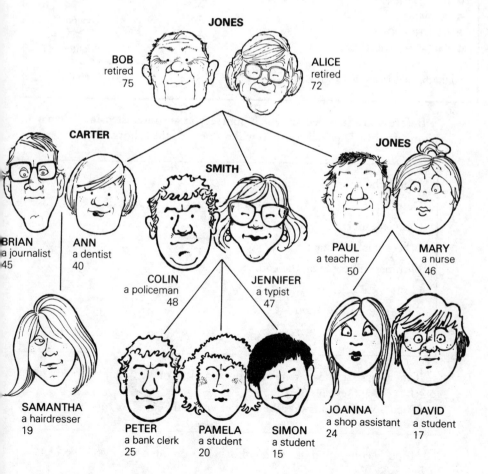

JONES

BOB
retired
75

ALICE
retired
72

CARTER

JONES

SMITH

BRIAN
a journalist
45

ANN
a dentist
40

COLIN
a policeman
48

JENNIFER
a typist
47

PAUL
a teacher
50

MARY
a nurse
46

SAMANTHA
a hairdresser
19

PETER
a bank clerk
25

PAMELA
a student
20

SIMON
a student
15

JOANNA
a shop assistant
24

DAVID
a student
17

19 Going on a weekend course

You live in London. You see the following advertisement in a magazine and decide to phone up WAY OUT WEEKEND COURSES for further details. (Student B works there.)

Way Out Weekend Courses

Looking for something different this weekend? Then try one of our popular weekend courses. Courses this month are:

- COMPUTER PROGRAMMING
- WATER-COLOUR PAINTING
- BIRD-WATCHING
- POTTERY
- FOLK DANCING
- WEAVING
- SELF-HYPNOSIS
- GHOST HUNTING

For further details phone 01-210 8091

Penrith
LAKE DISTRICT
YORKSHIRE
Manchester
Cambridge
WEST WALES
Tenby
London
Bristol
Brighton
ISLE OF WIGHT

Before you start, decide which course you are interested in. When you phone up, have a pencil ready to make a note of the following:

Where the course is being held: ....

Date: .... Number of days: ....

Course leader: ....

Where you will stay: ....

Number of people on the course: ....

Cost: ....

Any other information: ....

....

If the course sounds interesting, book a place on it. (Could I book a place on the course then, please?)

When Student B answers the phone, you can begin like this:

Good (*morning*). I'd like some information about one of your weekend courses.

20 Complete the drawing (1)

Here is a drawing of a kitchen with knives, forks, etc. Student B also has a drawing of a kitchen, but it is incomplete. Help him/her to complete it by telling him/her where the various things go. (The missing objects are shown under the drawing.) Student B is allowed to ask you questions, but he/she *must not see your book*. When you have finished, compare your drawings.

When you tell Student B where to draw the various things, you can use sentences like these:

> There's a clock on the wall between the two cupboards.
> There's a saucepan and a frying-pan on the cooker at the back. The saucepan's on the right and the frying-pan is on the left.

forks spoons knives saucepan bottle calendar vase breadknife

tea coffee clock teapot glasses jug cups saucers plates table cloth frying-pan

35

21 Complete the drawing (2)

On the opposite page is a drawing of a living-room. Under the drawing are a number of things which are to be found in a living-room (a vase of flowers, a painting, an ashtray, and so on.) Student B is going to tell you exactly where they are. When he/she tells you, draw them in the correct places. You are allowed to ask questions but you *must not look at Student B's drawing*.

When you have finished, compare your drawings.

You can ask questions like these:

> Where's the television set?
> Where are the glasses?

Here are some other questions you might ask:

> I didn't understand that. Could you say it again, please?
> Do you mean here?
> On which shelf – the one on the left or the one on the right?
> Which table do you mean? The coffee table or the small table next to the sofa?

bookcase

mantelpiece

armchair

coffee table

sofa

cat

picture

ashtray

spot light

magazine

clock

glasses

box of matches

painting

bottle

cushion

vase of flowers

vases

poster

television set

radio

lamp

book

22 Missing information: the life of Elvis Presley

A pop magazine has just started a new series called 'The History of Rock 'n' Roll'. Each week it presents a short life-history of a famous rock 'n' roll singer. On the opposite page is the life-history of this week's star – Elvis Presley. Unfortunately, some of the information about him is missing. By asking Student B questions, fill in the missing information. (Student B also has missing information and will ask you questions.)

Before you start, read through the life of Elvis on the opposite page and work out which questions to ask. For example:

> What was his father's name?
> What happened in 1942?
> What sort of job did he get when he left school?
> What was the name of the song he recorded in 1954?
> When did his mother die?

When you are both ready, you can begin. Take it in turns to ask and answer questions. *But you must not let Student B see your book.*

When you have finished, check to see if you have filled in everything correctly.

Full name: Elvis Aaron Presley

Parents: .... and Gladys Presley
Brothers/sisters: Jesse Garon (twin brother)
                    Died at birth

Year	Main event(s)
1935	Born in ...., Mississippi, on January 8th.
1942	....
1948	Moved to Memphis, Tennessee. Started at a new school. His father bought him ....
1953	Left school and got a job as .... with the Crown Electrical Company. That summer, he went along to Sun Records in Memphis and paid $4 to record two songs for ....
1954	Sam Phillips, the owner of Sun Records, asked Elvis to record a song called '..'. 20,000 people bought the record.
1955	Met Colonel Tom Parker. He became Elvis's manager.
...	Recorded a song called 'Heartbreak Hotel'. It sold over a million copies.
1957	Made more records – all of them were big hits. Became known as the 'King of Rock 'n' Roll'. He bought .... in Memphis which he called Graceland. Also went to Hollywood to make his first film – *Love Me Tender*.
1958	Went into the army and became a soldier in West Germany. On ...., his mother died.
1960	Left the army and went back to Hollywood to make more films.
1967	Got married to Priscilla Beaumont – a girl he had first met when ....
...	Appeared on a special television show. His daughter, Lisa Marie, was born.
1972	His wife, Priscilla, left him.
...	Elvis and Priscilla got divorced.
1977	Died of a heart attack at the age of .... on August 16th. He left all his money to .... 80,000 people turned up for his funeral and his records were played on the radio all day.
1978	100 million Elvis LPs were sold. The 'King of Rock 'n' Roll' was dead but certainly not forgotten.

23 Looking at holiday photographs (1)

The photographs on the opposite page are ones you took when you were on holiday last summer. You are going to show them to Student B. Talk to him/her about the photographs and about your holiday.

Before you start, think about things like the following:

(a) the photographs: where the photographs were taken the name of the building/place who the people are	*(b) the holiday:* where you went how long you stayed there who you went with what you did there what the weather was like

When you are ready, you can begin.
Start like this:

Would you like to see some photographs
of my holiday in ....?

Then show the photographs to Student B.

24 Newspaper interview (2)

Your name is Peter (or Susan) Webster.

You are a journalist. You work for the *Musical Express*. You are going to interview the manager of the American all-female pop group, Cheese (Student B). They became famous just over a year ago with their hit single, 'Wild Woman'. At the moment their manager, Paul (or Cathy) Storm, is in London making the final plans for their European tour which starts next month.

Before you start, work out some questions to ask, such as:

> When do you actually start your tour?
> How many countries are you going to visit altogether?
> When is the concert in London?
> Are you planning to do anything else while you are in Europe?
> How many records did 'Wild Woman' sell?
> Why do you think the group are so popular?

Try to think of other questions to ask. Find out as much as you can about the group and the tour.

When you are both ready, you can begin. You can start like this:

> How do you do, Mr/Miss Storm. My name's .... of the *Musical Express*. May I ask you one or two questions about your European tour?

And you can finish:

> Thank you very much for answering my questions and good luck with the tour.

25 Looking at holiday photographs (2)

Student B is going to show you some photographs he/she took while on holiday last summer. Try to ask lots of questions about them as well as questions about the holiday itself.

Here are some questions you can ask (think of others):

(a) about the photographs:

   Where was this taken?
   What's that building there?
   Who are these people? Do you know them?

(b) about the holiday:

   How long did you stay in . . .?
   Was it nice there?
   Who did you go with?
   Where did you stay?
   What did you do?

When Student B asks you if you would like to look at some holiday photographs, you can say:

Yes, that would be nice.

And when you have seen all the photographs, you can say:

They were very nice photographs. Thanks for letting me see them.

---

26 One-sided dialogue: shopping

Read the following dialogue with Student B.

Because you can see only your part, you must listen very carefully to what Student B says. Use the shopping list on the opposite page.

Before you start, read through your part to have some idea of what you will say. When you are both ready you can begin.

You:	Good morning. I'd like two pounds of sugar, please.
Student B:	. . .
You:	Yes . . . (*Ask for the second item on your shopping list*)
Student B:	. . .
You:	(*Ask how much the large packet is*)
Student B:	. . .
You:	(*Repeat the price*) I'll have a small packet then, please. And some apples.
Student B:	. . .
You:	(*Answer*)
Student B:	. . .
You:	Yes. (*Ask for a dozen eggs*)
Student B:	. . .
You:	Is there any difference in price?
Student B:	. . .
You:	(*Choose which eggs you want*) And have you got any tins of tomato soup?
Student B:	. . .
You:	(*Answer and say how many tins you want*) And a pint of milk. Is it still twenty pence?
Student B:	. . .
You:	Yes . . . (*Say you want some coffee*)
Student B:	. . .
You:	(*Ask what sort he/she has got*)
Student B:	. . .
You:	Which is the cheapest?
Student B:	. . .
You:	(*Say you will have a tin of that*)
Student B:	. . .
You:	Just one more thing – cheese. (*Ask if he/she has got any Cheddar cheese*)
Student B:	. . .
You:	Oh well – never mind. Right, how much is that, please?
Student B:	. . .
	(*Give Student B £10*)
Student B:	. . .
You:	Thank you. Goodbye.
Student B:	. . .

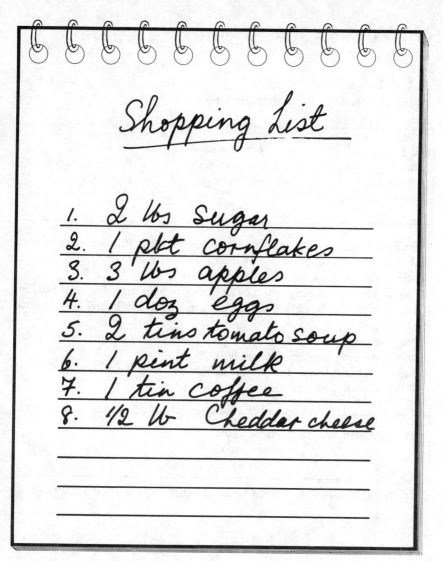

Shopping List

1. 2 lbs sugar
2. 1 pkt cornflakes
3. 3 lbs apples
4. 1 doz eggs
5. 2 tins tomato soup
6. 1 pint milk
7. 1 tin coffee
8. ½ lb Cheddar cheese

2 lbs = two pounds of   1 doz = a dozen
1 pkt = a packet of   ½ lb = half a pound of

(1 lb = approximately 0.5 kilograms)

27 Where's the station?

Look at the map on the opposite page. There are ten buildings which have not been marked. They are the following:

the car park	the post office	the café
the Chinese restaurant	the bookshop	the supermarket
the butcher's	the cinema	the baker's
the sweet shop		

Student B knows where these buildings are. Ask him/her questions to find out. When you know, mark them on the map. (Student B also has missing buildings and will ask you questions.)

(NOTE: The six buildings marked in black are on both maps, so if Student B asks you where the library is, you can answer, 'It's in Penny Lane next to the boutique.')

When you have finished, compare your maps to check that you have filled in all the missing buildings correctly.

Take it in turns to ask and answer questions. (Ask: Where's the . . .?)

When you answer, you can use sentences like these:

It's in (*Green Road*)	next to the . . .
	opposite the . . .
	between the . . . and the . . .
It's the (*first/second etc.*) building on the (*right/left*) in (*Penny Lane*).	

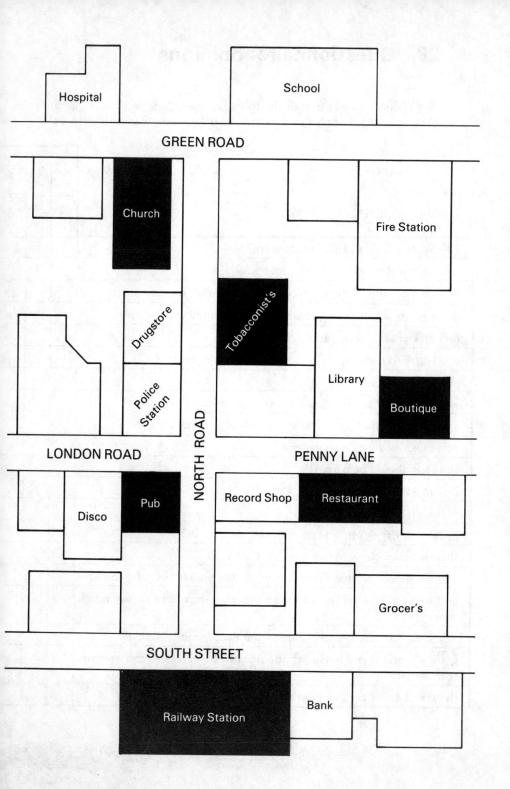

Hospital

School

GREEN ROAD

Church

Fire Station

Drugstore

Tobacconist's

Library

Police Station

Boutique

LONDON ROAD

PENNY LANE

NORTH ROAD

Disco

Pub

Record Shop

Restaurant

Grocer's

SOUTH STREET

Railway Station

Bank

47

28 Questionnaire: opinions

Work alone. Read through the following questions and choose an answer (Yes, I do/No, I don't/I'm not sure). Mark your answer with a cross (×).

Do you think . . .	Yes, I do	No, I don't	I'm not sure
English is a difficult language to learn?			
men and women can ever be equal?			
you can tell a lot about a person from the clothes he/she wears?			
the most important thing about a job is the money you earn?			
cats make better pets than dogs?			
it is better to grow up in the town than in the country?			
classical music is boring?			
you should not get married until you are at least twenty-five?			
a child should look after his/her parents when they are old?			
pop music is only for teenagers?			
smoking should be banned?			
it is an advantage to be an only child?			
politics is very interesting?			
people are happier nowadays than they used to be?			
there are such things as ghosts, UFOs, etc.?			
all men should be able to cook, sew, do the housework, and so on?			
pop stars, film-stars, sportsmen and sportswomen earn far too much money?			
watching television is more interesting than reading books?			
getting married and having children is more important for a woman than for a man?			
there will ever be a Third World War?			

When you have finished, work with Student B. Take it in turns to ask each other's opinions and to agree or disagree with them. Ask questions like these:

A: Do you think English is a difficult language to learn?
B: Yes, I do.
A: Yes, so do I. OR Do you? I don't. I think . . .

B: Do you think politics is very interesting?
A: No, I don't.
B: No, neither do I. OR Don't you? I do. I think . . .

A: Do you think men and women can ever be equal?
B: I'm not sure, really.
A: Oh, I do. OR Oh, I don't. OR No, neither am I.

(NOTE: If you disagree with Student B, try to give a reason for your opinion.)

29 Asking for information about a tour

You would like to go on a coach tour tomorrow with your cousin. You see the following advertisement and decide to phone up the London Travel Information Centre for more information. (Student B works as a clerk there.)

Coach tours

Daily coach tours to places of interest – including London tour.

● Brighton ● Isle of Wight ● Windsor Safari Park
● Oxford ● Stratford-upon-Avon *and lots of other places*

For further information, contact the London Travel Information Centre at Victoria Coach Station Tel. 01-730 0202.

If you find a tour that interests you, book two seats on it. Also make a note of the following:

Tour to ....

Leaves at ....

From ....

Cost ....

Arrives back at ....

When Student B answers the telephone, you can say:

Good (*morning*). I'd like some information about your coach tours. Which tours have you got tomorrow, please?

30 Asking for information about summer jobs

You work for an agency, Summer Jobs Agency, that helps students to find summer jobs. Student B phones you up for more information. Here are the jobs you have at the moment:

Job/place	Starting date	Length	Salary	Person to contact
Fruit picking (South of England)	June 15th	4 weeks	£60 per week	David Blake 01-210 8021
Waiters/Waitresses (Sunshine Holiday Camp, Scotland)	May 10th	6–8 weeks	£75 per week	Barbara Smith 01-210 8041
Guide (Battle Abbey, Battle)	June 1st	3–5 weeks	£50 per week	Anne Watson Battle 8021
Farm workers (Sunnydale Farm, Wales)	July 20th	5 weeks	£80 per week	Peter Watkins Swansea 8091
Cafeteria workers (DFDS Ferries: Harwich–Esbjørg)	July 1st	6–8 weeks	£90 per week	David Barker 01-210 8020
Youth leaders (Adventure Holiday Camp, Tampere, Finland)	May 29th	6–10 weeks	£70 per week	Helen North 01-210 8071

If Student B is interested in any of the jobs, give him/her the name and the telephone number of the person to contact. Also make a note of the following:

Caller's name: ....

Address: ....

Tel. No: .... Date: ....

Job recommended: ....

You can begin like this:

Good (*afternoon*). Summer Jobs Agency.

31 One-sided dialogue: an invitation

Read the following dialogue with Student B.

Because you can see only your part, you must listen very carefully to what Student B says. Use the diary on the opposite page.

Before you start, read through your part to work out what you will say. When you are both ready, you can begin.

You: . . . (*say your name or telephone number*)

Student B: . . .

You: Oh, hello, . . . (*say Student B's name*) How are you?

Student B: . . .

You: (*Answer*)

Student B: . . .

You: Yes, I'd love to. (*Ask Student B when he/she would like to go*)

Student B: . . .

You: On . . . (*repeat day*)? Oh, I can't, I'm afraid. (*Explain why*) But what about . . . (*suggest either Thursday or Friday instead*)? I'm free then.

Student B: . . .

You: Oh, good. (*Ask Student B what time*)

Student B: . . .

You: Yes, all right. Where shall we meet?

Student B: . . .

You: Yes, fine.

Student B: . . .

You: Yes, I'll look forward to it.

Student B: . . .

You: (*Say goodbye and thank Student B for telephoning you*)

Fill in your diary: Go to cinema with . . . Meet at . . . (*time/place*)

Your diary next week (evenings)

MONDAY

PLAY SQUASH   7.30

TUESDAY

VISIT UNCLE JAMES AND
AUNTY PAMELA   7 o'clock

WEDNESDAY

GO TO SALLY'S
PARTY   8.15

THURSDAY

FRIDAY

Appendix: Guide to the structures and functions used

Activity 1: Getting to know you (1)

Type of activity
Ice-breaker

Main structures
Present Simple – question and answer forms
Verbs: to be, have got, various others

Examples:
What's your name?
Have you got any brothers?
Where do you come from?

Main functions
Asking for and giving personal information
(see above examples)

Activity 2: Getting to know you (2)

Type of activity
Ice-breaker

Main structures
Various tenses – question and answer forms, including short forms (Yes, I am/No, I'm not, Yes, I do/No, I don't, etc.)

Examples:

Are you afraid of the dark?	Yes, I am/No, I'm not
Do you live in a town or a village?	(I live) in . . .
Have you got more than two brothers?	Yes, I have/No, I haven't
Can you swim?	Yes, I can/No, I can't
Were you born in May?	Yes, I was/No, I wasn't
Did you listen to the radio last night?	Yes, I did/No, I didn't
etc.	

Main functions
Asking and answering questions about yourself and others
(see above examples)

Activity 3: Missing information: the Eurovision Song Contest

Type of activity
Information transfer

Main structures
Present Simple – question and answer forms (verb *to be*)
             questions with *does*

Examples:
How old is Fleming Larsen?

54

Where does Marcel Meyer live?
Which country is 'Nana' singing for?
Is Paula Allen married or single?
etc.

Main functions
Asking for and giving personal information about other people
(see above examples)

Activity 4: Questionnaire: likes and dislikes

Type of activity
Questionnaire/discussion

Main structures
Like, love, don't like, etc. + noun
Like, etc. + gerund
So do I/Neither do I

Examples:

I like cats	Yes, so do I
I quite like writing letters	
I don't like washing my hair	No, neither do I
etc.	

Main functions
Expressing likes and dislikes (in varying degrees)
Agreeing or disagreeing with someone's likes and dislikes
(see above examples)

Activity 5: Who's who?

Type of activity
Information transfer

Main structures
Comparatives and superlatives of adjectives

Examples:
Peter is a year older than Sally.
The tallest person is a year younger than John.
etc.

Main functions
Asking for things to be repeated
Drawing conclusions
Asking for things to be confirmed

Examples:
Could you say that again?
So the girl on the left must be Sally.
Did you say that John is twenty-one next birthday?
etc.

Activity 6: One-sided dialogue: making suggestions

Type of activity
One-sided dialogue

Main functions
Asking for and making suggestions
Accepting or turning down a suggestion

Examples:
Shall we do something tomorrow?
How about . . .?
Why don't we . . .?
Let's . . .

No, I don't really like . . .
I'd rather not.
All right. Let's do that, then.

Activity 7: Following instructions (1)

Type of activity
Information transfer

Main structures
Imperatives
Prepositions of place

Examples:
Start in the black square.
Go to the square below the drawing of a house. In this square draw a large cross.
etc.

Main functions
Giving instructions
Asking for instructions to be repeated
Checking instructions

Examples:
I'm sorry, I didn't understand that. Could you say it again, please?
Did you say go left two squares?
etc.

Activity 8: Missing information: flats and houses

Type of activity
Information transfer

Main structures
Is there . . .?
Are there . . .?

Main functions
Asking for and giving information about flats and houses

Examples:
Where's the house?
Is the flat big?
Is the house modern?
How many rooms are there in the flat?
etc.

Activity 9: Following instructions (2)

See *Following instructions (1)*

Activity 10: This is my boyfriend/girlfriend

Type of activity
Simulation

Main structures
Question forms – various tenses
Questions beginning with a question word (*wh-* questions)

Examples:
Where did you meet him/her?
How long have you known him/her?
What's his/her job?
How old is he/she?
Do you plan to get married?
etc.

Main functions
Asking for and giving personal information
(see above examples)

Activity 11: Newspaper interview (1)

Type of activity
Role-play

Main structures
Future tenses – questions and statements

Examples:
When are you starting your march?
When do you hope to arrive in London?
Are you visiting many countries on the way?
What will you do about food?
etc.

Main functions
Asking and answering questions about future plans
(see above examples)

Activity 12: This is my brother

Type of activity
Simulation
(see *This is my boyfriend/girlfriend*)

Activity 13: Questionnaire: habits and daily routines

Type of activity
Questionnaire

Main structures
Adverbs of frequency – always, usually, often, etc.
'Do' questions

Examples:
Do you go out at weekends?   Yes, always
Do you remember your dreams?   No, not often
Do you find it easy to make friends?   Yes, usually
etc.

Main functions
Asking and answering questions about habits and daily routines
(see above examples)

Activity 14: For sale

Type of activity
Simulation

Main functions
Describing things (a cassette recorder)
Asking and answering questions about something (a cassette recorder)

Examples:
What make is it?   It's . . .
How much do you want for it?   About . . .
Does it have a radio?   Yes, it does.
etc.

Activity 15: Eye-witness

Type of activity
Role-play

Main functions
Describing someone (physical appearance)

Examples:
How old was he?
How tall was he?
Was he fat or thin?
What colour was his hair?
What was he wearing?
etc.

Activity 16: Complete the crossword

Type of activity
Information transfer

Main functions
Asking for and giving definitions of words

Examples:

What's 6 down?
What's 10 across?
etc.

You eat it. It's a fruit. It's yellow.
It's the opposite of 'hot'.

Activity 17: Carry on talking

Type of activity
Role-play

Main structures
Past tense – questions and answers

Examples:
Where did you go?
Were you alone?
What did you do?

Why didn't you phone me to let me know you weren't coming?
What was the party like?
Who was there?
etc.

Main functions
Talking about a pleasant event
Giving explanations
Talking about a party
(see above examples)

Activity 18: A family tree

Type of activity
Information transfer

Main structures
Present Simple – question word + verb *to be/have got*

Examples:
Who is Bill married to?
Is Paul a teacher?
How many children have Colin and Jennifer got?
Is Samantha nineteen?
etc.

Main functions
Asking for and giving personal information about people
Asking for confirmation that something is true
Saying that something is not true

Examples:
Who is Mary married to?   She's married to Paul.
Is Samantha a hairdresser?   Yes, that's right.
Is Pamela a shop assistant?   No, she's not. She's a student.
etc.

Activity 19: Going on a weekend course

Type of activity
Simulation

Main structures
Would like . . .
Question word + verb *to be*
                    + *will*

Examples:
I'd like some information about one of your weekend courses.
Where is it being held?
How much does it cost?
etc

Main functions
Asking for and giving information about a course
(see above examples)

Activity 20: Complete the drawing (1)

Type of activity
Information transfer

Main structures
There is . . .
There are . . .

Where is . . .?
Where are . . .?

Prepositions of place

Examples:
There's a clock on the wall between the two cupboards.
There are three cups in the cupboard on the right.
Where's the jug?   It's . . .
Where are the glasses?   They're . . .
etc.

Main functions
Saying where things are in the kitchen
Asking where things are in the kitchen
Asking for something to be repeated
Asking for confirmation

Examples:
(see above examples)

Also:
I didn't understand that. Could you repeat it, please?
Do you mean here?
In which cupboard – the one on the right or the one on the left?
etc.

Activity 21: Complete the drawing (2)

As above, except that this activity is about saying where things are in the living-room.

Activity 22: Missing information: the life of Elvis Presley

Type of activity
Information transfer

Main structures
Past tense – questions with *did*
Past tense – *wh-* questions

Main functions
Asking for and giving information about a person's life
Narrating past events

Examples:
Where was Elvis born?
What happened to him in 1942?
What job did he get when he left school?
When did his mother die?
etc.

Activity 23: Looking at holiday photographs (1)

Type of activity
Simulation

Main structures
Questions and answers – Past tense

Main functions
Asking and answering questions about a holiday
Describing photographs

Examples:
Where did you go for your holiday?
How long did you stay in . . .?

Was it nice there?
Who did you go with?

What's this building here?
Who are these people?
Where was this photograph taken?
etc.

Activity 24: Newspaper interview (2)

See *Newspaper interview (1)*

Activity 25: Looking at holiday photographs (2)

See *Looking at holiday photographs (1)*

Activity 26: One-sided dialogue: shopping

Type of activity
One-sided dialogue

Main structures
I'd like + *some* + noun (countable, uncountable plural)
        + quantity + noun
Have you got . . .? + *any* + noun
How much + noun (uncountable)
How many + noun (plural, countable)

Examples:
I'd like two pounds of sugar, please.
Have you got any tins of tomato soup?
How much does it cost?
etc.

Main functions
Stating what you would like to buy
Asking how much of something someone wants
Inquiring about prices, brands, etc.
(see above examples)

Activity 27: Where's the station?

Type of activity
Information transfer

Main structures
Where is + building
Prepositions of place

Main functions
Asking about, and saying, where buildings are

Examples:

Where's the hospital?	It's in Green Road opposite the Chinese restaurant.
Where's the pub?	It's the first building on the left in London Road.
etc.	

Activity 28: Questionnaire: opinions

Type of activity
Questionnaire/discussion activity

Main structures
Questions beginning with Do you think . . .?
Yes/No answers   (Yes, I do/No, I don't/I'm not sure)
So do I/Neither do I

Main functions
Asking for and giving an opinion
Agreeing or disagreeing with an opinion
Stating uncertainty

Examples:

Do you think English is a difficult language to learn?	Yes, I do.	Yes, so do I. Do you? I don't.
Do you think politics is very interesting?	No, I don't.	No, neither do I. Don't you? I do.
Do you think men and women can ever be equal?	I'm not sure, really.	No, neither am I. Oh, I do. Oh, I don't.

etc.

Activity 29: Asking for information about a tour

Type of activity
Simulation

Main functions
Asking for and giving information about a tour

Examples:
I'd like some information about your coach tours.
Which tours have you got tomorrow, please?
When does the tour to Brighton leave London?
Where does the coach go from?
How much does it cost?
When does the coach get back to London?
Could I book two seats for the tour to Brighton, please.

Activity 30: Asking for information about summer jobs

As above, but this time asking for information about summer jobs.

Activity 31: One-sided dialogue: an invitation

Type of activity
One-sided dialogue

Main structures
Would you like to + verb phrase
What about + noun
When + *shall* + verb

Main functions

Asking how someone is (and answering)
Giving an invitation
Accepting an invitation
Turning down an invitation with a reason
Suggesting an alternative day
Arranging a time and place to meet
Confirming arrangements

Examples:

Hello, . . . How are you?   I'm all right, thanks. And you?

Would you like to go to the cinema with me next week?
Yes, I'd love to.
On Friday?   Oh, I can't, I'm afraid. I have to . . .

What about on Thursday? I'm free then.
Yes, Thursday would be fine.

What time?
Where shall we meet?

Right, I'll see you on Thursday, then.
Yes, I'll look forward to it.

Picture Credits